M000287890

The Prayers of Others

David Keplinger

03-04-07

To Steven,
Hope you enjoy
some of these
poems.
Thanks for
your interest
in my work.

David

New Issues Poetry & Prose

A Green Rose Book

New Issues Poetry & Prose
The College of Arts and Sciences
Western Michigan University
Kalamazoo, Michigan 49008

First Edition, 2006.

ISBN-10   1-930974-63-9 (paperbound)
ISBN-13   978-1-930974-63-0 (paperbound)

Library of Congress Cataloging-in-Publication Data:
Keplinger, David
The Prayers of Others/David Keplinger
Library of Congress Control Number: 2006924616

Editor   Herbert Scott
Copy Editor   Curtis VanDonkelaar
Managing Editor   Marianne Swierenga
Designer   Steven Tagsold
Art Director   Tricia Hennessy
Production Manager   Paul Sizer
                            The Design Center, School of Art
                            College of Fine Arts
                            Western Michigan University

The Prayers of Others

David Keplinger

New Issues

WESTERN MICHIGAN UNIVERSITY

Also by David Keplinger

For Michael and Kathryn Franzoni

Contents

Here may be seen how being blessed
Has its foundation in the act of sight,
And not in love, which comes afterwards . . .

Paradiso XXVII, 109-111

I STOOD TOO CLOSE to the lion cage and was eaten right up. My mother called and called for me. I left no trace above. I landed in the lion's gut, and the gut was melted butter; its kills strung high along the cursive of its vertebrae. When the lion breathed in deeply, they flapped. I named this purring.

ON THE FIRST level of Hell with Francesca and Paolo sits Max Jacob. You had no choices; Francesca says to Paolo. You had no choices, says the other to the other. Jacob in his dirty pin stripe suit just laughs and laughs at them. He has a brief affair with one of Darwin's finches. She visits only at night. She permits him to stroke the yellowish down of her breast, which occasionally he reads by.

LIFE ON EARTH is pulled down hard on a man's head. This life was made by hatters. A busy street is only coffee, bread, and hats. The smell of a man's hat—an old man's hat—is like the nostril of a horse. You are breathing in what something beautiful and ancient has breathed out. The heat and life contained in it, the silk interior. An old man's hat is necessary: You see that when he takes it off, his hair and skin abruptly float away.

IT WAS OLD, the joke the man told, in which a man has lost his overcoat. It made another man begin to laugh. And so they calmly waited in the stairwell in the dark. For who could imagine the building would go down, or that the one who laughed would not survive? "Only by shattering can we attain our perfect form," the ancients said. The man who died could not stop laughing.

WALKING BY MYSELF through cities I think of knives, the symbol of marriages and doom. Or I recall the lucky spoons my auntie loved and hung on a rack by the table. She did not love her knives. They lay in the drawer. My auntie ripped her bread by hand. She said a knife is almost useless, being one thing only.

POEMS WITH EXCLAMATION POINTS! Poems composed by circus clowns! Shy poets of America, that's just what we need: a vaudeville kind of poem, with a girl to read the titles from a placard on the stage. Titles like: How I Became a Poet! Or: Richard Nixon Pees in China! Or: Hot Night in Duluth! The kind that drench the audience with seltzer!

I WAS A FABULOUS city-state bedeviled by an earthquake and a war. You were my guardian in the temple. All the soldiers on their parapets had tumbled into the sea. They were turning into dolphins. Their penises shrank into feeble contrivances. Even you couldn't save them, who were off somewhere helping Achilles to carefully strap his sandals.

MY FATHER IS a nine-year-old, leaning on the deep iron sink in the kitchen. His father guts a fish. His mother stands in the dark of the hallway, the one light showering her short brown hair. Her face is grimaced, to make the little boy laugh. The tiny heart and eggs are gleaming in his father's hand: easily distinguishing what's this from that.

THIS IS A FARCE. But a dangerous farce, with streamers and fireworks that sometimes set the stage ablaze. The main players are a shrew, a doctor, and a princess who never appears. She's ill. The doctor has gone to see her. He returns with a mask: "Distress." The shrew, the only interesting one, throws her black confetti in the air, then sweeps it immediately up.

THE CLOTHESLINE where the fugitive hung his prison shirt. A finch came and stood on the shirt's bloody shoulder. All night it stood there. The people in the house got up and made the beds. The father hammered something in the upper room. The shirt hung on its little equals sign between the house and open field, one sorrow and another.

NIXON PEED ALL OVER Mao Tse Tung's best toilet bowl in China. A servant caught him as he tried to clean the blunder up. The Chinese snickered collectively when he boarded the plane to leave: How did they find out? he asked himself. The pee became a national joke. It was so yellow, they said, Americans must live on corn alone.

THE SEPHARDIM KNEW their secrets would have to wait for Max Planck, for Heisenberg, for Schrödinger to be born. Meanwhile we don't care about the emptiness. We want to touch. This is what we want: to press this face into the other face. The light and heat aren't waves at all, but heavy, thick as paint. Everything is fixed and long-decided.

EVERYWHERE IN HELL are sad mosaics. Despite your distance, no matter how you squint, no picture comes to mind from all the shattered bits. The theme, of course, is Cubist. Where the Wrathful and the Sullen live, there are whole critics' circles devoted to analysis. But mostly they complain, run their hands along the glass, and lick their fingers.

THE LITTLE GIRL has turned away her eyes, covered up her face as if ashamed. In this picture she has chanced upon a rotting cow. The giant teeth exposed, its mouth has burned away like film burns in a theater. Her shadow fills a little scrap of fur against the belly of the thing, wet like turf in darkness. She has to pose the hurt—the caption notes—to fetch that smile out of the other.

MY FATHER SLAMMED his brake to meet a hairpin curve, and sent us gliding on the ice, and out of God's care. The Buick carried me, my mother in her giant fur, my sleeping sister, my father in his suit and overcoat, his stiffened, dry-cleaned shoulder. Someone on the radio began to sing. Death-of-self, like a song I'm still in love with, singing, you are that little gasp of breath.

STORMS WERE PASSING OVER US. All summer mangled baseballs turned up smashed in bales of hay. Her father found out everything: our feather arrows and our letters and the redwing shot through the eye. I have to say this like I'd say it through a keyhole. It was far too dark to see into her room across the field, where he had taken her.

THERE IS THE WOMAN who washes the stairs. She was a beauty once, but now has lost her beauty. She's stopped here a moment to place her ear against the door of my room. The stairs are quiet, except for her rag that scratches into the gravel. And down she continues to go. Her bucket of soap is the first to turn black, before she does.

WHEN I WENT off to war, I stopped to visit the tombs that lay in the Fourth Circle. One of the voices I heard was my teacher's. He was dabbing the sores on his mouth with a cloth. What right do you have to speak of a war? he asked. "I'm only dreaming this, and you are still alive," I tried to tell him. The cloth was not cloth; it was his teacher's face.

THE PRISONER WOULD JACK himself off all night; all day he'd wander through the yard like Teresa with the mark of God upon her forehead. That lyric striving rushing always towards story, towards death-of-self, towards resolution, it did him little good. His visions turned up splashed into the mattress; made him sleepy; got him nowhere fast.

I KEPT NO DOLLS in my doll carriage but a loaded tool belt, heavy as a child. Each metal instrument developed a personality. The pliers were afraid of flat surfaces. I'd talk to them the way a mother soothes her crying babes. "Since the Fall there is a job for everyone," I told these pliers, which lulled them right to sleep.

MILTON, BLIND and useless, visited the office of employment in Malebolge. He'd had it with paradise, this sitting around doing nothing to the tunes of Petrarch. There is no devil as we've come to think. In the offices and offices of clerks, each desk job has a stamp that snuffs the paperwork of one door down.

I WATCHED A MAN insert his whole grown body into a small glass box. With a flourish he dismantled and fell limp inside. Is that all this is? How small a box is my lifetime? How large, please, is a human being? The man was smiling. He sat behind the X his legs had marked, unsocketed.

WHERE I SHOULD have come to Judas impaled by huge incisors, instead I discovered Antonin Artaud, still writing his manifesto, "To Finish with the Judgment of God." All his teeth were pulled. It was so quiet there, I even heard the scratching of his pen. He had no jacket for the long-approaching winter. A kind of dog had chewed his hands and feet.

COULD THIS BE SATAN, whose drop from Heaven made this hole? I thought to myself. It was a tiny child, hanging by four straps, like the heart suspended on its branches. That baby's just a memory: My mother had left me to swing in the shade.

TIME IS MOVING exactly at the pace a girl can read by candlelight. And when she mouths the words, running her finger under the words as she speaks them, tadpoles burst into frogs, a liver regenerates, flesh rises off the body as a fleck of dust. She never stops, except when her eyes get tired, and that's when we notice the silence.

MY FATHER CLIMBED his ladder to the roof, his tool belt hanging at the waist. Up there I'd tossed a little toy I loved; I threw it with my might; I swung it on its purple string, let go. The toy, a soldier, wouldn't float back down. It landed in the gutter and was stuck. My father knelt at the gutter edge and almost lost his footing: this thing of little value in his hand.

HOW MANY SPARROWS am I worth? A sparrow of the kingdom *Animalia,* of the *Aves* class, foraging for seed and maggots, somewhere in the sweating reeds along the Nile. I held a sparrow once. I saw no difference from a finch; the stout, unending chest; the supercilium in bold; the curtness of its beak and brains. Light who clothes me, I ask you.

THE OLD MEN AT THE Y when I was twelve would pace the locker rooms without their towels. A mushroomy pud and balls hung shriveled within every crotch. To see them in their disrepair, unashamed, complaining of their money and the blacks, made stripping difficult and sad. The eldest wore a small, white rag atop his head.

BETWEEN THE TENEMENTS the flowery housedresses and giant panties flutter. The place is narrow—two arm lengths, best—where lines are fashioned across this alley, twenty stories high. Today the wind is light and spring has come. The passing cars in traffic only get a glimpse. Way up a pair of hands is passing cake into another pair of hands. Their garments touch each other lavishly.

AGAINST THE OLD-fashioned mesh of the radio the barber pressed his good ear. He was still holding a small, white cloth for covering the face. The cloth was hot. Steam was rising from it. In and out the static hissed like someone shushing children. His heart in his ear, which no one else could hear, made the sound that boots make through the snow.

DON'T LEAVE ME for the afterlife again. Don't go into exile again. Don't lift that window with the blackbirds on the ledge. Don't sip for hours your greasy wine. Well, it's too late. Your lips are disappearing, your face. The birds are gathering in trinities. See, and off they go.

HAVING HIDDEN SO LONG beneath the corpses of our parents, we were children with gray hair when we pushed their bodies away. There was a hurried emigration for a distant country. We stood along the platform, waiting. We heard the heavy digging of the engine. The train had actually come on time! Conductors helped us upward by the arms.

INSTEAD OF RAIN, it poured green horseflies, eardrums, teabags, and the complete works of Sigmund Freud. Luckily we had the awning up. Our conversation on the triune structure of the brain was not disturbed. "We are part reptile, part ape, part fool," she said. Just then *Jokes and Their Relation to the Unconscious* knocked down all the wine from out of nowhere.

THE OLD MEN HAVEN'T CHANGED at all, but I have. In clean white shirts they sing about their lives. That one who looks so sad, he could be my Uncle Joseph. His own son wouldn't come to his funeral. He's too sensitive, the widow said. All my life I've ached to hear that tone in me. When it comes I'm never ready. It comes when I have nothing much to say.

WE BARELY SAW the mirror through the mailslot of the barber shop. We had to strain our eyes. The mirror and the shop were dark. Where were the secret drawers for razor blades and gum? The human skull and its phrenologies? Where was the naked goddess of the calendar? Her umbrella flying backwards in her hands?

HERE IS THE SLAG HEAP in Shamokin, Pennsylvania. By now its filmy crust has sprouted grass the roughness of a husk of corn. The heap has made them famous: and so came Vaudeville, Talkies, and the USO. Underneath, the whole thing smolders, like the center of the earth has jutted out. You can't climb up, though boys that drowned in it have tried.

EVERY LITTLE CLASSROOM has its Emily. This one calls the cross "the stake." Imagine her Lord beleaguered like that, the mythic crucifix merely vertical. She never has a thing to eat. When she finally collapses, she awakens to our worried faces. Later she's back at her desk in her trance. She clasps her hands into a sphere. She knows the shortcuts through the fields that we don't know.

WE STRIPPED and swam to the Green Island. It was earliest summer. There is such a thing as midnight sun. Asa let me touch her from behind, her body so much older than mine. Under water she yelled something—what? I don't remember. What we call "sorrow" is merely failing memory.

EVERY PARTICLE OF MATTER is a Christ: each one come from nothing to be something. The portions tell a different aspect of the story. The horses, for example, with their heads in séance, illustrate the final moments of his life: the sad glance down. The stone: his face with eyes closed. The eel: his spirit swimming up.

A SWIMMING COMPETITION in the afterlife. The dead have arrived, wearing their blue trunks. We watch them from our bodies on the shore. Their faces, bright doubloons. The dead are pure buoyancy; their struggle is to stay submerged. We have to cheer them on, or you know what: These swimmers simply float into the sky.

KEPLER KNEW the earth contained a soul. He saw the fossils written on the stones as blueprints for the "shaping forces." Archeopteryx, half bird, half dinosaur, might have driven him to curses. Its tasseled head like one of Bosch's devils; its chicken claws; the strictness of its here-nor-there.

HE WAS TRYING TO BREED a kind of rabbit whose liver might be soft enough to stuff with ease into the ribbony intestines. The white ones were his latest. Their jaundiced eyes were only calmed when he took up his trumpet and performed for them. The wife came barging in. "She doesn't like the music," he told the rabbits glumly, and played a little more.

AT THE CORNICE I find Nietzsche fast asleep, his Kaiser's mustache puffing in and out. A glass of tonic settles on his bedside table. His stomach has started to rumble. In his dream, captured in a bubble in the tonic glass, he's arguing the Will with John the Baptist. The head speaks from a plate of foods that never have agreed with him.

THE CORPSE IN ITS BEAUTIFUL CLOTHES: does another image, even Christ's, relate an equal mystery? Of the kingdom we know little. The body and its folded hands are sad. All mystery is sad, my friend once said, age after age. And dying of his cancer, he was sad. A sadness lacking target or a range. His reveries were ordinary danger.

ADAM'S ON THE RIGHT, his name is Red Earth. His face is burned, as if made of ash. He lies on his back on the sand, a tree growing out of his sex. The tree contains all metals known to us. The branches spread like veins into the dirt and cities and the rivers of the world. He gives us choice: to be the anvil or the sword.

EVE STANDS ON THE LEFT. Her belly, pouched, is a pelican's mouth. She is neither mercurial nor shy. She clasps a fish in one hand, a cloud in the other. Look closely now: the fish is not a fish. Above her are the sun and moon, even in the sky. Her cloud is full of lightning bolts that strike like serpents touching mouths.

ONLY THE PRAYERS of others can save me. Likewise, mine save only them. The little girl who lost her tooth went looking for it through the house. Had she swallowed it last night? Her thinking and the house were large. She flung a piece of string, as though to lasso the tooth, as though it were a loose, wild beast that must be tamed. We'd do anything to comfort her.

MOTHER SANG the words to a song that made men love her. What song that was, or where she'd learned it, I don't know. The music carried to The Barn of Norristown and all the polka bars in Conshohocken. The song was scratchy on the record. "That's the crackle of the heart," she belted out, to the tune of a basic arpeggio.

O DYING-OF-THIRST NOMAD of ancient Arabia, you're going to have to learn to use your sword for chopping lettuce in the next life. And housing's tight. You'll room with a citizen of Atlantis. The drowned will sleep on top bunk; and you will sleep on bottom. That's a little gift: His dripping clothes will mean a constant source of rain.

THE CATS OF ROME come with the Pope into the afterlife. It is his punishment for all the Galileo business. In his antechamber, some sunlight filters through the portiere. It looks just like the Vatican in 1632. With one difference: instead of servants, the cats crowd in as he disrobes. They have no leader. He shushes them at length in the vernacular.

A JAR OF PEACHES, brought in by your mother. To wake up famished after surgery. Your father in his work clothes pining there. There. Your mother on the left side, sitting by the telephone. Your father on the right, beside the clock. Their prayer like a little song. You remember it clearly. The shriek inside the accident. The jar of peaches turning in your mother's hands. These things you ache to say. Reject the glue of rhetoric, which seeks the antidote to pain.

THE MOST LOVELY of the horses in my grandmother's livery has died—a white stallion she washed with a dripping sponge each morning. You have to imagine, she said, the rippled neck all muscular, tense, flop earthward, to awaken in wonder at what it had been. You'd have to picture how the yogi's rope, when he climbs down, collapses.

BECAUSE HE LOVES his new wife George, William Yeats fakes his automatic writing. There is a story of his process of revision: It isn't automatic enough, he says. They live in the tower at Thor Ballylee; her dream horses leap from their parapets; everyone's eyes are closed. Of course, Yeats is down in the stable in his dream, gathering hay and sugar cubes.

A RED-WINGED cousin of a firefly, without luciferin, landed on my book. "Take care, take care," the book had said. The insect's face had fallen out of heaven. Whatever falls from heaven in its own way says, "No shit." No parts of it were longer than an eyelash. With its forelegs it wiped one feeler down, the way a boy wipes down a spear.

MARIA CAME BACK to fetch her little dog, who was tied up to the tree for all these years. Since she had died it wouldn't come inside. The dog had yapped and snapped at neighbors and refused to be consoled, so there it sat until she came for him. It was like you see in silent film: the beautiful, robed woman and the winter tree, clearly filmed on two locations.

THE EAR'S AN EARTHY GARDEN with its own forbidden tree: God still walks there leisurely in the cool of the evening. The tree has never been discovered. That's why the garden stinks of rinds; the swells of full fruit thudding in our heads. "The porches of my ears," Dead Hamlet called its tiny gate, its nautilus design, where someone's often whistling.

AT EXACTLY THIS spot in the room, she said, whenever I pass through it, this location, facing the wall, facing the window with its light like today's, I have to lift my hands up to my face and cry. The dark spot in the wooden floor—a knot? An imperfection? This was where it always happened. Like standing on the planet Mercury, she said: that hot, bald stone.

THE WAY IT WAS DONE, every vital organ but the heart was placed in canisters to stay alive. The heart was left to die inside the body. Years it lay within that velum membrane, perfumed of natron, the excess soups, the blood and bile. Immortal life must be *attained,* they said. It's not a given that the heart is lonely and so must live forever.

I AM an actor playing myself, walking my grandfather down the road. He is an actor, too, the most distinguished of them all. He wants to speak. The words barely flicker on his throat's wick. *Write it down, Write it down,* I tell him. I hold this man by the thick of the arm, its muscle of wool. And he exits: he and his small white papers.

VENUS IS A BALL of gas that, underneath, has mountains like the Catskills. The only blessed souls that live there are Romantic poets and, in special cases, toxic frogs, St. George's dragon, and the angel whose job it is to visit us in dreams. The angel would like to give the job to Keats, who is too busy taking labored breaths into his handkerchief.

MY GRANDFATHER instructed me: He stood in his pressed white shirt and then got shy, and so did I. But it was simple. He clicked the music on and clasped my hand. Open up and move with it, he said. The waltz is dactylic: undertow, undertow, undertow. I hadn't learned that rhythm yet. When I recall these urgent lessons, this is how I think.

"THE HIDDENNESS of God is necessary. It's like the space between a thing and other things. Without it there could be no urge to go forth, and we are here to go forth. What we discover at the moment of our death is this: There is no space between a thing and any other thing. And God is not hidden, just as there is no going forth."

The Prayers of Others

David Keplinger

THE ONLY LIFE from Mars we know of are the geese who travel back and forth to it perpetually. Their gladiator arrow, which pointed to that speck of glitter in the sky, was not the pivotal detail. Two things suggested they were not like us. The first was lacking chain in their command. Next was how they'd pair themselves: the injured with the well.

HE COULD SEE the clock from any angle in the house: but regardless where he stood it told a different time. From the window, for example, the clock appeared an hour slow. By the door it was fast. And if he woke up in the middle of the night and walked into the darkness of the hall, it had no hands, though he could hear it, clearly ticking through the hollow of the rooms.

ON OUR FIELD TRIP to the planetarium, Mrs. Watson pointed out the seven spheres, explaining for each its virtue. When a soul came down from heaven, she said, it gathered up the light to form a body. The sad curator raised his head out of the book. He tapped his watch and whispered: "Time." Underneath her sweater when she spoke her breasts would sway.

AFTER THE RAIN the prison yard was empty. The prisoners remained in their cells reading the collected works of Kant. One of them stood up, as if standing outside his body, as if watching himself turn gingerly a yellowed page. The only curtain now between this man and Nothing? The welt of pleasure thumping in his head.

.

IN HER HOSPITAL BED, mother drinks her water from a plastic cup. They have stolen me under their coats so I can visit her. They've made a show of it. She sits up straight and strong in her chair. Memory's like skipping stones. I'm in the lobby with my Coke. I'm carried to the room where light pours in. Her face as blurry snapshot when she smiles from under her handkerchief.

I'VE BEEN TO THIS STATION, but will never go back. A beautiful woman in a green gown was clasping a shoe to her ankle. The stiletto on that shoe the length of my pointer finger. Her other foot was bare. The woman stood up, threw her purse on the crook of her shoulder. *Tik-tump, Tik-tump,* and away she went. The train pulled out. Tell me, what shall I do with that image? The woman's still there. She walks on the stilt of my finger.

I MADE THIS paper boat for her, who finds it difficult to sleep. She imagines she is floating on its little stern, here, under her sleeping mask, under the covers. All you'll need is one plain sheet. It's folded like the beak of some archaic bird. With your fingers pry the wide beak open. You are opening the beak. You are climbing inside.

Acknowledgements

The author would like to thank *The Iowa Review,* in which "Life on earth . . .", "Between the tenements . . .", and "I've been to this station" first appeared (as "In Palermo") and *Copper Nickel,* which printed the following pieces: "This is a farce . . ." "I kept no dolls . . ." "I watched a man . . ." "The corpse in its beautiful clothes . . ." "At the cornice . . ." "Nixon peed all over . . ." "The prisoner would jack . . ." "I was a fabulous . . ." "A red-winged cousin . . ." and "Against the old fashioned . . .".

Thanks to the National Endowment for the Arts, the department of English at CSU-Pueblo, and to my friends at WWLD: Rebecca Laroche, Aaron Anstett, Jane Hilberry, Jake York, and Jenn Koiter, as well as to dear friends Bill Sheidley, Bill Varner, Anissa Solano and Jennifer Richter for their diligent attention to early drafts of this book.

Finally, my gratitude to Herb Scott, editor at New Issues, whose comments and confidence have made all the difference.

photo by Lisa M. Nelson

David Keplinger's second poetry collection, *The Clearing*, was published in 2005. His first book, *The Rose Inside*, won the 1999 T.S. Eliot Prize. He has received grants and awards from The National Endowment for the Arts, the Pennsylvania Council on the Arts, the Soros Foundation, and the Katey Lehman Foundation. His poems, essays and translations have appeared in *Ploughshares, Poetry, AGNI, Gettysburg Review, Prairie Schooner, The Iowa Review,* and many other journals. Keplinger directs the creative writing program at Colorado State University—Pueblo.

New Issues Poetry

Vito Aiuto, *Self-Portrait as Jerry Quarry*
James Armstrong, *Monument in a Summer Hat*
Claire Bateman, *Clumsy; Leap*
Kevin Boyle, *A Home for Wayward Girls*
Michael Burkard, *Pennsylvania Collection Agency*
Christopher Bursk, *Ovid at Fifteen*
Anthony Butts, *Fifth Season; Little Low Heaven*
Kevin Cantwell, *Something Black in the Green Part of Your Eye*
Gladys Cardiff, *A Bare Unpainted Table*
Kevin Clark, *In the Evening of No Warning*
Cynie Cory, *American Girl*
Peter Covino, *Cut Off the Ears of Winter*
James D'Agostino, *Nude with Anything*
Jim Daniels, *Night with Drive-By Shooting Stars*
Joseph Featherstone, *Brace's Cove*
Lisa Fishman, *The Deep Heart's Core Is a Suitcase*
Robert Grunst, *The Smallest Bird in North America*
Paul Guest, *The Resurrection of the Body and the Ruin of the World*
Robert Haight, *Emergences and Spinner Falls*
Mark Halperin, *Time as Distance*
Myronn Hardy, *Approaching the Center*
Brian Henry, *Graft*
Edward Haworth Hoeppner, *Rain Through High Windows*
Cynthia Hogue, *Flux*
Joan Houlihan, *The Mending Worm*
Christine Hume, *Alaskaphrenia*
Josie Kearns, *New Numbers*
David Keplinger, *The Clearing; The Prayers of Others*
Maurice Kilwein Guevara, *Autobiography of So-and-So: Poems in Prose*
Ruth Ellen Kocher, *When the Moon Knows You're Wandering;*
 One Girl Babylon
Gerry LaFemina, *The Window Facing Winter*
Steve Langan, *Freezing*
Lance Larsen, *Erasable Walls*
David Dodd Lee, *Abrupt Rural; Downsides of Fish Culture*
M.L. Liebler, *The Moon a Box*
Alexander Long, *Vigil*
Deanne Lundin, *The Ginseng Hunter's Notebook*
Carrie McGath, *Small Murders*
Barbara Maloutas, *In a Combination of Practices*
Joy Manesiotis, *They Sing to Her Bones*
Sarah Mangold, *Household Mechanics*
Gail Martin, *The Hourglass*
David Marlatt, *A Hog Slaughtering Woman*

Louise Mathias, *Lark Apprentice*
Gretchen Mattox, *Buddha Box; Goodnight Architecture*
Paula McLain, *Less of Her; Stumble, Gorgeous*
Lydia Melvin, *South of Here*
Sarah Messer, *Bandit Letters*
Wayne Miller, *Only the Senses Sleep*
Malena Mörling, *Ocean Avenue*
Julie Moulds, *The Woman with a Cubed Head*
Marsha de la O, *Black Hope*
C. Mikal Oness, *Water Becomes Bone*
Bradley Paul, *The Obvious*
Katie Peterson, *This One Tree*
Elizabeth Powell, *The Republic of Self*
Margaret Rabb, *Granite Dives*
Rebecca Reynolds, *Daughter of the Hangnail; The Bovine Two-Step*
Martha Rhodes, *Perfect Disappearance*
Beth Roberts, *Brief Moral History in Blue*
John Rybicki, *Traveling at High Speeds* (expanded second edition)
Mary Ann Samyn, *Inside the Yellow Dress; Purr*
Ever Saskya, *The Porch is a Journey Different From the House*
Mark Scott, *Tactile Values*
Hugh Seidman, *Somebody Stand Up and Sing*
Martha Serpas, *Côte Blanche*
Diane Seuss-Brakeman, *It Blows You Hollow*
Elaine Sexton, *Sleuth*
Marc Sheehan, *Greatest Hits*
Heidi Lynn Staples, *Guess Can Gallop*
Phillip Sterling, *Mutual Shores*
Angela Sorby, *Distance Learning*
Matthew Thorburn, *Subject to Change*
Russell Thorburn, *Approximate Desire*
Rodney Torreson, *A Breathable Light*
Robert VanderMolen, *Breath*
Martin Walls, *Small Human Detail in Care of National Trust*
Patricia Jabbeh Wesley, *Before the Palm Could Bloom: Poems of Africa*